FOR THIS I WENT TO COLLEGE?

by

Bil Keane

FAWCETT GOLD MEDAL • NEW YORK

FOR THIS 1 WENT TO COLLEGE?

Copyright © 1974 by The Register & Tribune Syndicate

© 1977 CBS Publications, The Consumer Publishing
Division of CBS, Inc. All rights reserved

A Fawcett Gold Medal Book published by arrangement with
The Register & Tribune Syndicate, Inc.

ISBN 0-449-14069-5

Printed in the United States of America

14   13   12   11   10   9   8   7   6   5

¡"Mommy! Guess what it did outside last night!"

"The boots bit off my shoes again."

"You can go in there to talk to Mommy. She's just changing her clothes."

"Isn't there anything good to eat?"

"Mommy, will you take out yesterday's knots so I can put my shoes on?"

"Don't let me win too easy, Daddy."

"I didn't LOSE my sweater — it's SOMEPLACE! I just can't remember which place."

"Look what Jack Frosting put on our window!"

"We just wanted to know what you're doing."

"Why did that man call me 'son'? HE'S not my daddy."

"Slow down, Billy! We're drivin' over 55!"

"Mommy has an upset head."

"Guess what those spell."

"I wish the robins would get here so winter would be over."

"Will somebody come here and close my covers, please?"

"Wanna play, Daddy? It isn't too hard."

". . . and so the poor doggie had none."

"So she had to phone and get a pizza for him! Right, Mommy?"

"Oh, no! They sold our bus stop!"

"Daddy, my balloon popped. Will you blow it up again, please?"

"You were closer this time, Grandma, but it's not a cow, it's an airplane."

"Dolly knocked the vase over, but it's okay 'cause the couch caught it."

"I thought this was 'sposed to be a POCKET dictionary!"

"What was I going to say, Mommy? I forget."

"That one has the prettiest roof."

"Not now — Daddy's tired. Go ask Mommy."

"I wondered why so many girls had curls today and it was 'cause we had our pictures taken."

"Mommy! Dolly's losing her temperature!"

"How come these drawings I made for you are goin'
out with the old papers?"

"Mommy! I think it's somebody!"

"I don't like tea. Let's make believe it's somethin' else."

"The picture was already there. I only colored it."

"I think somebody's tired and ready for bed." "Yes, and it's Billy."

"This mirror looks back at me, but why won't it ANSWER like in 'Snow White'?"

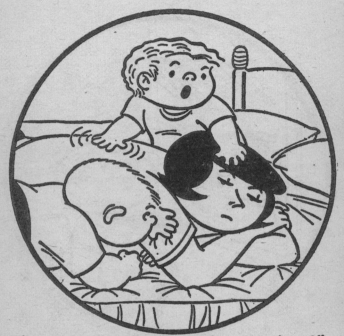

"Mommy, will you let us know when you wake up?"

"Daddy, will you show me how to play baseball?"

"We have to take pictures of presidents to school
I'm taking the dollar Grandma gave me."

"Did you stub your head?"

"Dummy! Planes don't beep!"

"You shouldn't walk in front of busses like that, lady."

"I forgot to tell you today's your turn to be lunch room mother at 12 o'clock."

"Will you turn the radio off, Mommy? My singing is getting all mixed up with their music."

"I am SO as tall as you, Billy! Look!"

"Mommy, will you come and lie down with me? I feel
unattentioned."

"We had intelligence tests today. Boy! Were they
HARD!"

"They're playin' 'Ring Around the Collar'."

"Daddy says he's gonna buy steel-belted radios for the car."

"My name's on backwards!"

"Grandma wrote 'Wm.' on my envelope. Is that an old-fashioned way to spell 'Billy'?"

"It sure is a puddly day."

"Cause they were too crowded in the bowl."

"Can't we go to a store where they have TOYS?"

"We all got new clothes for Easter except Daddy.
He's just getting a haircut."

"Are you home, God?"

"Daddy won't let me help him paint!"

"I can't skate on the sidewalk yet, Daddy, but I'm doin' good at walkin' on the grass in 'em."

"Mommy, Dolly went from 'twosies' to 'fivesies'. Is that right?"

"It's raining! Quick! Turn on the wish-washers so I can see!"

"Tomorrow is Sunday and that means the SUN will be out all day."

"I didn't say Billy could listen to my book!"

"Guess what! When the one and the two sit down together, it's a TWELVE!"

"Wow! Look at Jeffy's plant grow! He's a very good mother."

"Daddy said I could have some cookies — how many
is 'some'?"

"I'm gonna eat my dinner so all-gone you won't even
recognize it!"

"Our regular teacher was sick today, so we had a sitter."

"Hi, Barfy's mother!"

"Daddy, do you want me to eat your pudding so you
won't have to?"

"The McCauleys have their wading pool set up already!"

"Why did you cut my squash in half, Mommy? Now I have TWICE as much to eat."

"Did God put out his lights
early to save 'lectricity?"

"If you had gotten me started at this when I was younger, Daddy, I'd be REALLY good by now."

"If you don't play cards with me,you'll be sorry 'cause
I was gonna let you win."

"Come quick, Mommy! PJ made a tragedy!"

"Daddy just yawned and we're all passin' it around."

"We invented a neat game! It's called 'kill the guy with the ball'."

"Hereafter I go jogging alone."

"Come on in and see what my grandma can do
she's tying knots in a string with two sticks."

"Can we have a doggy bag for the mints?"

"You're giving me a hair-ache!"

"Daddy, when we're washin' the car should the windows be up or down?"

"Jeffy must be very happy — everything he draws is smiling."

"It's a TENT, Mommy! Can we sleep outside tonight?"

"Can we get in it now, Daddy?"

"It's almost dark, Mommy. Shouldn't you and Daddy
be gettin' into the house now?"

"Don't lock the back door 'cause somebody might
want to come in and see what time it
is or somethin'."

"NOW how many hours till it's mornin'?"

"After breakfast I think I'll take a nap in my bed."

"Can I wear my cowboy hat, too, Mommy?"

"Grandma, can you tie a hole in this rope?"

"Boy! Mommy's gonna be RICH!"

"Stop that wastin', Jeffy! Don't you know there's an oil shortage?"

"I have a surprise for you, Daddy. Close your hands
and hold out your eyes."

"I was just sittin' here taking my bath and Sam came
walkin' along and FELL IN!"

"We're late 'cause we had to stand and talk to a lady you and Daddy know—the one with all that long yellow hair and the very short dresses."

"It's not fair! You always play at the deep
end and put me in the shallow part!"

"There are some words you can't use in front of childrens or mixed-up company, right, Mommy?"

"Tim Walsh's mother cleaned out their basement
and gave me all this neat stuff."

"You made a mistake and got some on the ceiling, Daddy. Are you goin' to erase it?"

"Jeffy wants you to hear something, Grandma."

"I know where his shoes are. He put them in the hamper 'cause they were dirty."

"Mommy! The paint's dry already! See,
I didn't get a bit on my hand!"

"But it was just a PLAY rock!"

" ... and you're to tell Mrs. Morgan you're sorry
and you'll never throw rocks again and you'll
pay for it with money you earn!"

"Mrs. Morgan, Jeffy has something to tell you. Jeffy?
What have you to say? Speak up — Jeffy, what
are you going to tell Mrs. Morgan? Jeffy?"

"I sorry."

"This came today. It's the bill for replacing the Morgans' broken window."

"Daddy, what does #X*X)#!! spell?"

"Shh! Don't interrupt! Mommy's talkin' to her plants!"

"Grandma, I'll let you read me just ONE MORE story."

"Poor Mommy! There isn't a single picture in your book."

"I CAN'T look up — the sky keeps gettin' in my eyes."

"Does flour come from REAL FLOWERS?"

"Say when."

"You're not S'POSED to understand. They're talking in politics."

"When I grow up to be a mommy, I'll be able to change a light bulb, too."

"I said 'front seat' first!"

"Mommy, y'know what you came down with when
we were suspectin' PJ? Well, now I think Mrs. Monroe
caught it."

"That's a very polite can."

"Mommy! Dolly's using up all the cold."

"Oh, no! Dolly brought 'tato chips instead of the tennis balls!"

"Doesn't your family have another car?"
"No, our car is an ONLY car."

"First I was small like a baby, then I grew up into a kid."

"Don't bother with MY clothes, Mommy. I like to go around unironed."

"Daddy fell asleep, but the TV is still awake."

"Close your eyes, Jeffy — I'm comin' in."

"PJ is younger than me and Billy is older. That makes me MIDDLE-AGED!"

"Don't YOU kiss me goodnight, Dolly — you'll mess up Mommy's kiss!"

HAVE FUN WITH THE FAMILY CIRCUS

I'M TAKING A NAP	M3413	95¢
LOOK WHO'S HERE!	M3419	95¢
PEACE, MOMMY, PEACE	M3417	95¢
PEEKABOO! I LOVE YOU!	M3418	95¢
WANNA BE SMILED AT?	M3332	95¢
WHEN'S LATER, DADDY?	M3411	95¢
MINE	M3370	95¢
SMILE!	M3517	95¢
JEFFY'S LOOKIN' AT ME!	1-3688-4	95¢
FOR THIS I WENT TO COLLEGE?	1-3829-1	95¢
CAN I HAVE A COOKIE?	M3375	95¢
THE FAMILY CIRCUS	M3374	95¢
HELLO, GRANDMA?	M3401	95¢
I CAN'T UNTIE MY SHOES!	M3310	95¢
I NEED A HUG	M3402	95¢
QUIET! MOMMY'S ASLEEP!	1-3930-1	$1.25